D1809175

BYZANTINE FABRICS

THE WORLDS HERITAGE OF WOVEN FABRICS

Other volumes are to follow and will be announced from time to time

BYZANTINE FABRICS

by

CYRIL G. E. BUNT

F. LEWIS, PUBLISHERS, LTD.
LEIGH-ON-SEA

Byzantine Fabrics

IN THIS SURVEY of the World's Heritage of Woven Fabrics so important a place is taken by the products of the Byzantine weavers that it behoves us to try to visualize the relations existing between Byzantium and her neighbours during the momentous epoch when the Eastern Roman Empire held a prominent position. Following Gibbon scholars have been persuaded to think of the Byzantine ages as one of decline. But in fact the age does not reveal any such decadence, except as temporary dips in the graph of alternating rise and fall of a general series of epochs of brilliance.

Commencing with the date 330 in the fourth century, when Constantinople became the capital of the Roman Empire, we may say that, when the Greek-speaking East was separated from the Latin-tongued West, the divorce was absolute. Whereas in the course of two centuries the West was subjected to barbarian influence and became crude in culture and in politics chaotic, the East retained its sophistications and, in art, as in its religion, it triumphed.

Justinian (527–565), in the sixth century, in his attempt to resuscitate a Mediterranean Empire, succeeded in the creation of a Greek state whose art, like its politics, was a brilliant barrier between the Islamic and the Romanesque of mediaeval Europe. Another epoch of brilliance occurred in the eighth-ninth centuries and, after a decline in the tenth, saw in the two following centuries a revival under the Comnenian dynasty (1057–1185) and for a second time the Byzantine Empire was again a barrier against the growing influence of Islam.

Thus the events of a thousand years left the Grecian Empire with a proud heritage of culture, which has been the wonder of the world, 'the nurse, protector and educator of the infancy of Western Civilization', to use the words of Professor G. B. Smith, in a lecture delivered thirty years since.

Justinian's reconquest of Italy has its due effect upon the textile, as upon the other arts, and the indebtedness of the West may be observed in the emergence of well-known textile patterns (of Byzantine derivation) in Italian weaves as well as those of other areas of contact.

The Byzantine world, during this and even subsequent times, is linked with the main trends of development and, because of its cultural heritage, the silks both in design and technique exhibit a relationship in place where the dominant influence had made itself felt.

Italy, upon which the mantle of silk fell from Byzantine shoulders in the tenth century, was perhaps the most important of its recipients. Miss Wiebel* has pointed out that there was a considerable and profitable contraband trade during that century, both in raw and woven silks.

From the tenth to the twelfth century the rich fabrics woven upon the Imperial looms of Constantinople and Antioch had impinged (to their great advantage) upon the alert craftsmen of Venice, Amalfi, Lucca, and the Islamic weavers of Egypt, North Africa, and hence Peninsular Spain.

With the fall of Constantinople in 1445, the renaissance was so far advanced that the fragments of the older culture were greedily absorbed in England, France, Germany and, above all, in Italy. In addition, with the final destruction of the Hellenic Empire and the cultural barrier between East and West, the Byzantine influence was so strong that it did not succumb. Through the Orthodox Church it spread to all the arts of Tsarist Russia and, in a lesser degree, of all the Slavic lands. Even in far-distant France the Eastern influence was discernible in the enamelling of Limoges.

It has been chronicled elsewhere in this series that Iran had close contacts with the Byzantine Empire. Its textiles were distinguished by similar decorative motives, notably the characteristic roundel enclosing addorsed animals, natural or mythic, heraldic devices and so forth. While it is not yet proven when originally derived, it is generally allowed that the Sassanians obtained the roundel from Byzantine sources, even if they did not get the simple twill technique from the same source as they obtained the silk-thread to make the rich garments which they so much esteemed.

Whatever country imported woven silks there was the Byzantine type to inspire their custom and, whether the influence is readily discernable or not, there was scarcely a port on the whole Mediterranean which did not know of the rich Byzantine silks. France particularly was a lucrative customer. The Greeks were installed in Narbonne in the sixth century. The city's concilliary reports of the year 589 mention at least five nationals among the population – Goths, Romans, Syrians, Greeks and Jews – while Ebersalt states that Marseilles and the cities of Provence were points of departure for the spread of Hellenism in Gaul, while at the same time he refers to the commercial contact between France and Byzantium and thus with the Orient.

*Adèle Coulin Weibel, Curator of Textiles, The Detroit Institute of Art

Thus it may be seen how very important the Byzantine culture is to the whole question of the formative influences at work in the development of European fabrics.

We see therefore that the spread of art influences was dictated by geography. A glance at the map of Europe at the period will show that the important centre in ancient times was Antioch, where was a concentration of luxury merchandise. It was supplanted by Constantine's Constantinople, which made itself paramount in the East while in close touch with the West.

It was the fusion that this infers between East and West which was the basis of all Byzantine art. The Hellenic or Greek spirit contributed the quality of delicacy, Semitic or Eastern contacts gave it strength and force. And the strength of this concentration is demonstrated in the rich collections which are still extant at the present day. There was on the one hand the diplomatic relations giving the occasion for sumptuous presents by diplomats and emissaries. On the other hand, there was the normal trade contacts. Both bring about the change of outlook and taste which assimilates the character, the design, and the general features of the original products. The permanent character of the resulting style inferred by the term 'influence' is at times hard to distinguish. Such influences are discernable by comparative study of the specific examples given in the appropriate volumes of this series, which is the chief reason why in this particular instance it has seemed appropriate to give a brief chronological account of the connection in Byzantine textiles between the prolific East and the continually progressive West.

ILLUSTRATIONS

Fig. 1 QUADRIGA SILK. 6TH CENTURY
Courtesy, the Cathedral, Aachen (Aix-la-Chapelle)

Fig. 2   SILK TAPESTRY. ALEXANDRIA, c. A.D. 500
Courtesy, the Cluny Museum, Paris (photograph from CIBA Review)

Fig. 3   WOVEN SILK PANEL. HITHER ASIA OR ALEXANDRIA. 6TH CENTURY
Courtesy, the Victoria & Albert Museum, London

Fig. 4   WOVEN SILK ROUNDEL (FROM AKHMIM).
HITHER ASIA OR ALEXANDRIA. 6TH CENTURY
Courtesy, the Victoria & Albert Museum, London

Fig. 5   SILK DAMASK, PERSIAN (SASSANIAN) 6TH–7TH CENTURY
Courtesy, the Victoria & Albert Museum, London

Fig. 6   SILK, WITH ORNAMENTAL LOZENGE PATTERN. 6TH–7TH CENTURY

Fig. 7 (top)   VINE PATTERN SILK. ALEXANDRIA.
6TH–7TH CENTURY
Courtesy, the Cathedral, Aachen (Aix-la-Chapelle)

Fig. 8 (left)   SILK WITH MONOGRAM OF EMPEROR HERACLIUS.
A.D. 610–614
Courtesy, the Cathedral Church of Liege

Fig. 9 (right)   LOZENGE PATTERNED SILK. 6TH–7TH CENTURY
Courtesy, the Cathedral Church of Liege

Fig. 10   SILK, HUNTING PATTERN IN PERSIAN STYLE. c. A.D. 600
Courtesy, the Diocesan Museum, Cologne (From the Cunibert Reliquary)

Fig. 11   SASSANID 'HORSEMAN' TAPESTRY. 7TH CENTURY
Courtesy, Palace Museum, Berlin. (photograph from CIBA Review)

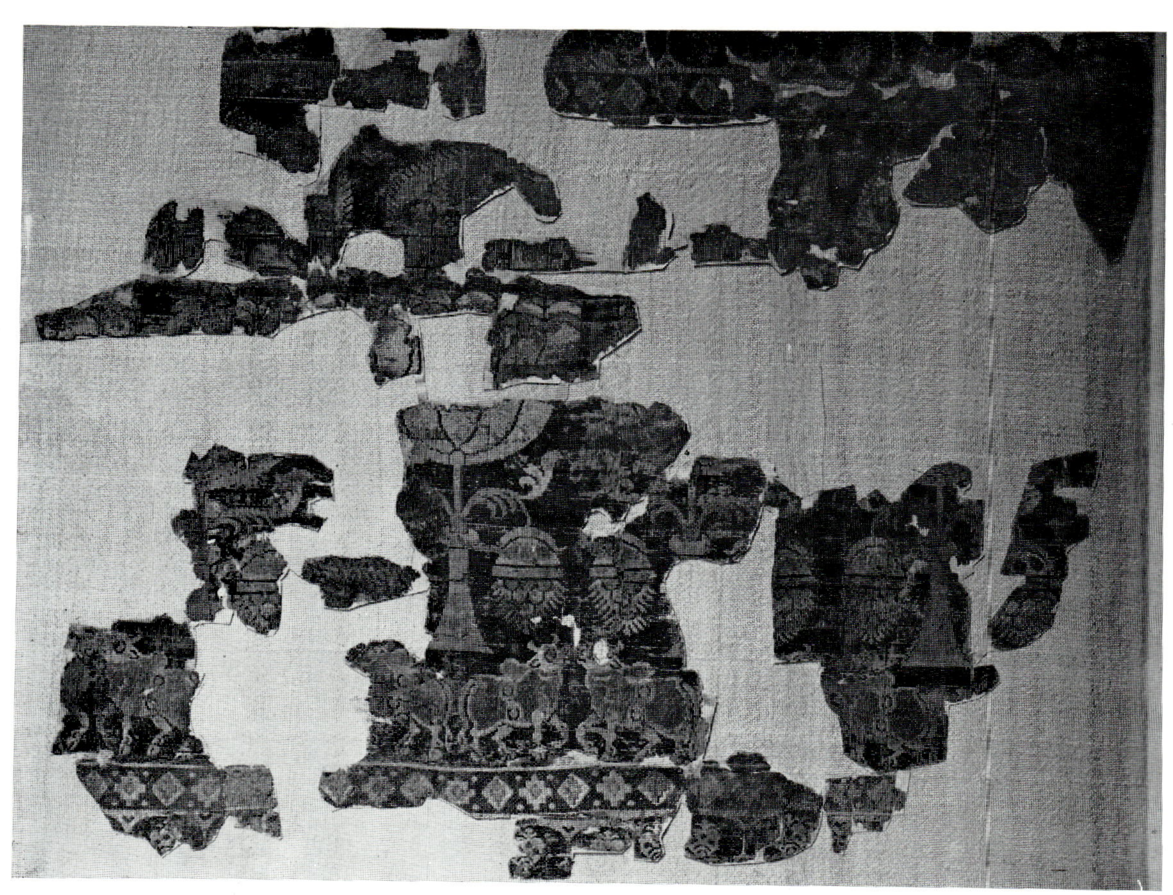

Fig. 12   TAPESTRY FRAGMENT WITH "TREE OF LIFE"
AND TWIN BULLOCKS (SASSANIAN). 7TH CENTURY
Courtesy, Musée Historique des Tissus, Lyon

Fig. 13   SHROUD OF ST. VICTOR. 7TH–8TH CENTURY
Courtesy of the Cathedral, Sens

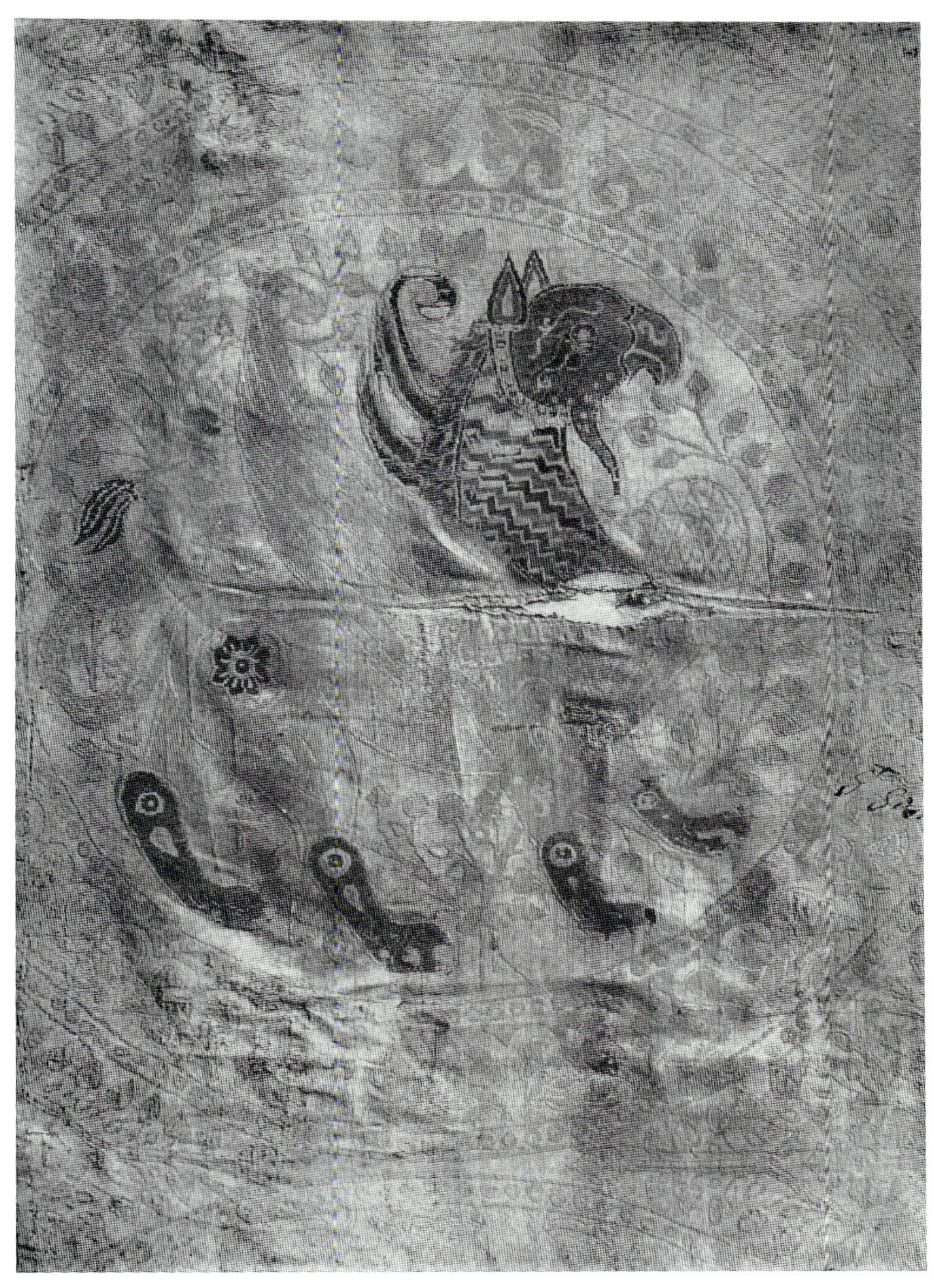

Fig. 14   SHROUD OF ST. SIVIARD. 7TH–8TH CENTURY
Courtesy of the Cathedral, Sens

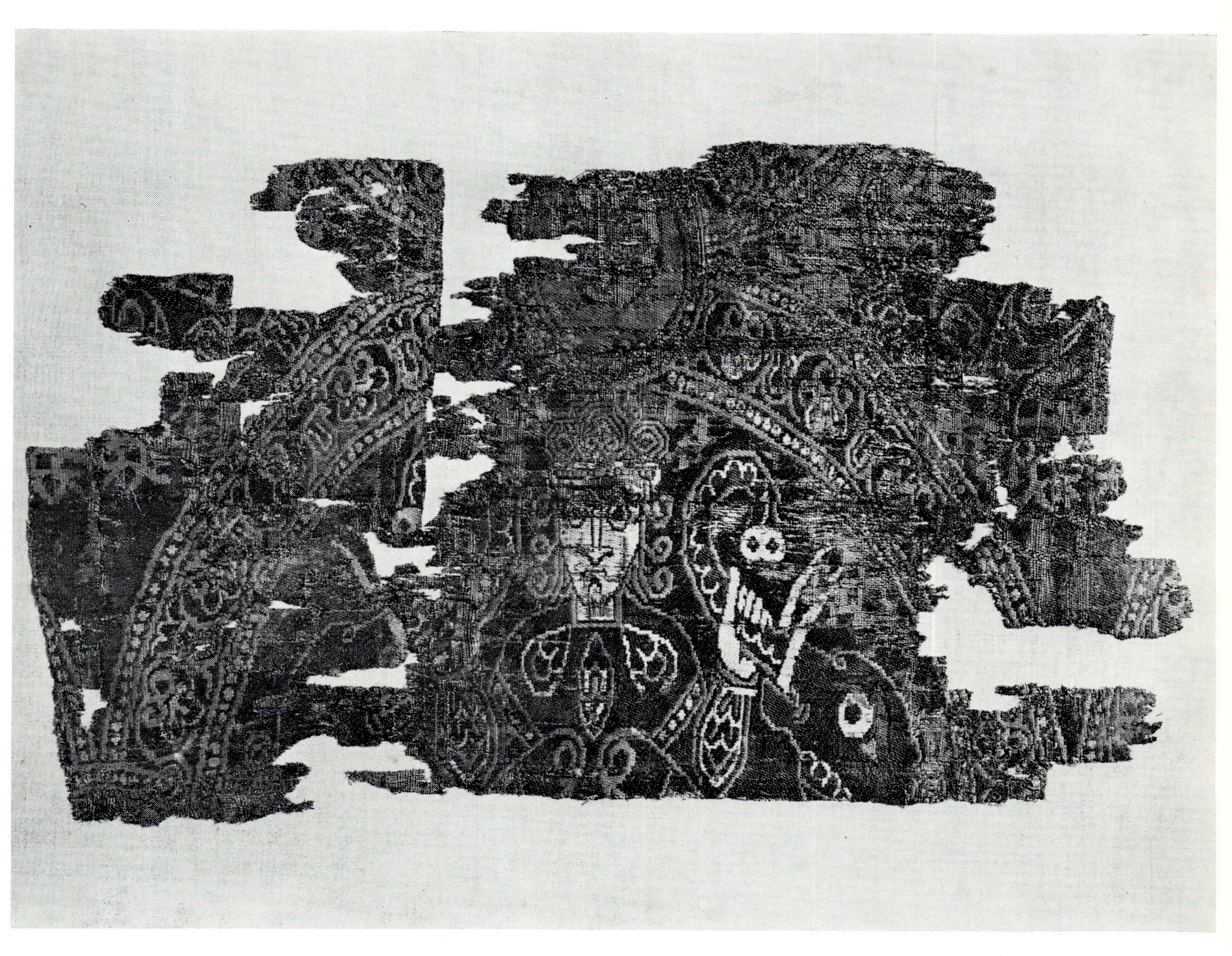

Fig. 15   ELEPHANT TAMER SILK. 7TH–8TH CENTURY
Courtesy, The Dumbarton Oaks Collection, Harvard University

Fig. 16   "BAHRAM" SILK. 7TH–8TH CENTURY
Courtesy, Schlossmuseum, Berlin

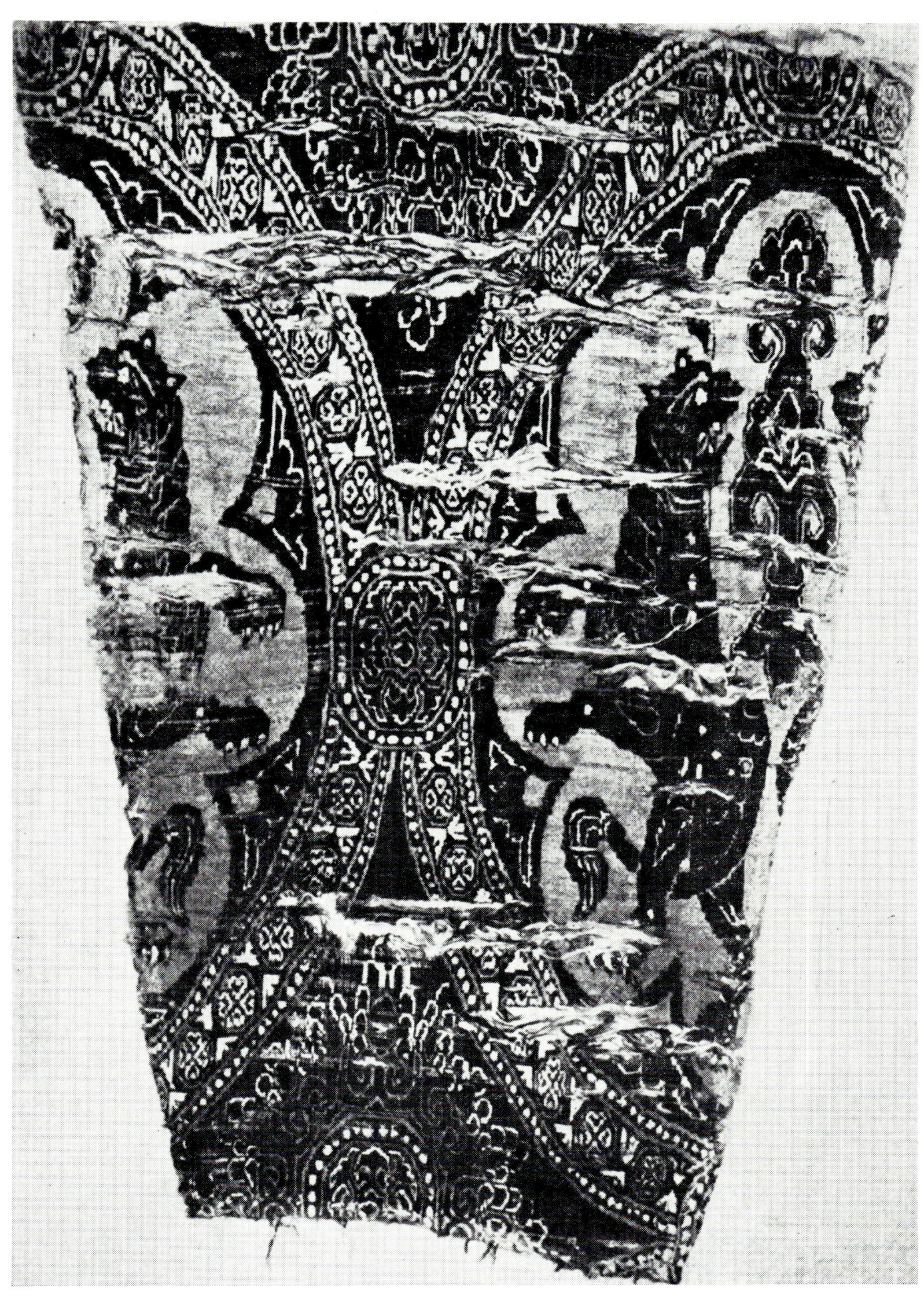

Fig. 17   ADDORSED LIONS, SILK. 7TH–8TH CENTURY
Courtesy, Musée de Valère (Valais), Switzerland

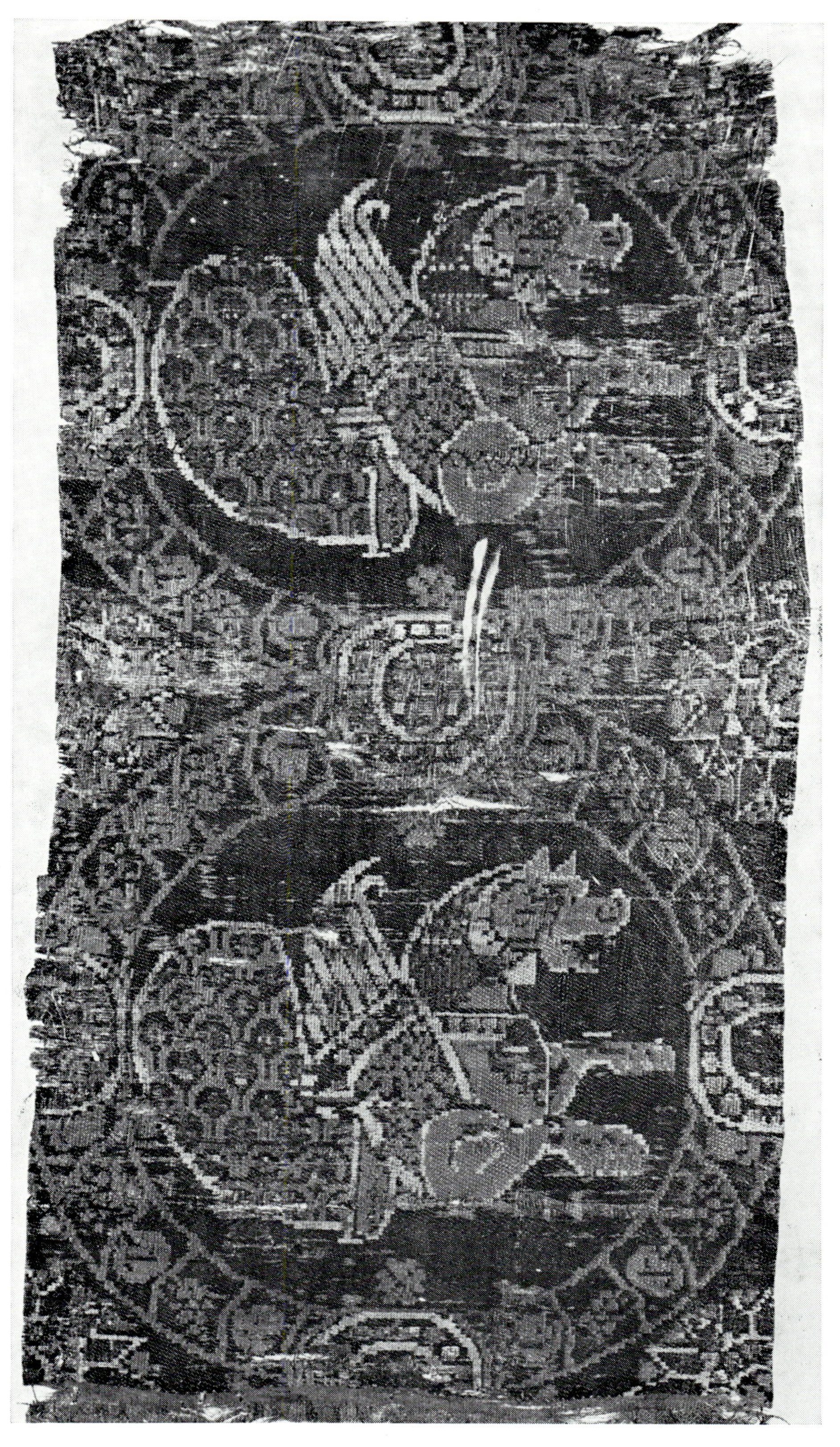

Fig. 18 PLAIN COMPOUND WEFT TWILL. SILK.
BYZANTINE VERSION OF SASSANIAN MOTIF. 7TH–10TH CENTURY
Courtesy, Cooper Union Museum, New York, U.S.A.

Fig. 19   "LION STRANGLER". SILK COMPOUND TWILL. 7TH–8TH CENTURY
Courtesy, the Victoria & Albert Museum, London

Fig. 20   SILK WEFT TWILL. GRYPHON PATTERN. 2ND HALF 8TH CENTURY.
Said to have come from the tomb of Viventia, daughter of Pepin the Short
Courtesy, Museum of Fine Arts, Boston

Fig. 21   PLAIN COMPOUND WEFT TWILL, SILK. 8TH–9TH CENTURY
Courtesy, Cooper Union Museum, New York U.S.A.

Fig. 22   "THE ANNUNCIATION". c. A.D. 800
Courtesy, Museo Sacro, Vatican City, Rome

Fig. 23   PLAIN COMPOUND WEFT TWILL. SILK. 8TH–9TH CENTURY
Courtesy, Cooper Union Museum, New York, U.S.A.

Fig. 24   STRIPED GRYPHON PATTERN. 8TH–10TH CENTURY
Courtesy, Church of St. Martin, Liege

Fig. 25 PLAIN COMPOUND WEFT TWILL. SILK. 8TH–11TH CENTURY
Courtesy, Cooper Union Museum, New York, U.S.A.

Fig. 26 EMPEROR IN FULL STATE DRESS DRIVING A
QUADRIGA. SILK FRAGMENT. 9TH CENTURY
Courtesy, the Victoria & Albert Museum, London

Fig. 27   SILK. FROM THE ABBEY OF MOZAC. 9TH CENTURY
Courtesy, Musée Historique des Tissus, Lyon (photo: CIBA Review)

Fig. 28 (left)   DOUBLE-HEADED EAGLE PATTERN. 10TH–11TH CENTURY
Courtesy, Kunstgewerbe Museum, Berlin

Fig. 29 (right)   IMPERIAL SILK WITH EAGLE PATTERN. 10TH–11TH CENTURY
Courtesy, Knuds Church, Odense, Denmark

Fig. 30 COMPOUND TWILL, SILK. 10TH CENTURY
Courtesy, Museo Nazionale, Ravenna, Italy

Fig. 31 (left)   SILK STOLE. 10TH–11TH CENTURY

Fig. 32 (right)   SILK. 10TH–11TH CENTURY

Courtesy, Victoria & Albert Museum, London

Fig. 33 (top)   ST. WILLIGIS CHASUBLE. SATIN WEAVE WITH INSCRIBED PATTERN.
10TH–11TH CENTURY *Courtesy, Mainz Cathedral*

Fig. 34 (bottom left)   ST. ULRIC'S CHASUBLE. INSCRIBED PATTERN, SILK.
10TH–11TH CENTURY *Courtesy, Augsburg Cathedral*

Fig. 35 (bottom right)   ST. EBBO'S CHASUBLE. INSCRIBED SILK. 10TH–11TH CENTURY
Courtesy, the Cathedral, Sens

Fig. 36   SILK. 10TH–11TH CENTURY
Courtesy, Victoria & Albert Museum, London

Fig. 37   PEGASUS COMPOUND TWILL. 10TH–11TH CENTURY
Courtesy, Kestner Museum, Hannover

Fig. 38. (top) LION PATTERN. MADE IN IMPERIAL WORKSHOP
IN THE REIGN OF CONSTANTINE VIII AND BASIL II (A.D. 976–1025)
(Photograph from CIBA Review, Basle)

Fig. 39 (bottom) LION PATTERN. 10TH–11TH CENTURY
Courtesy, Kunstgewerbe Museum, Berlin

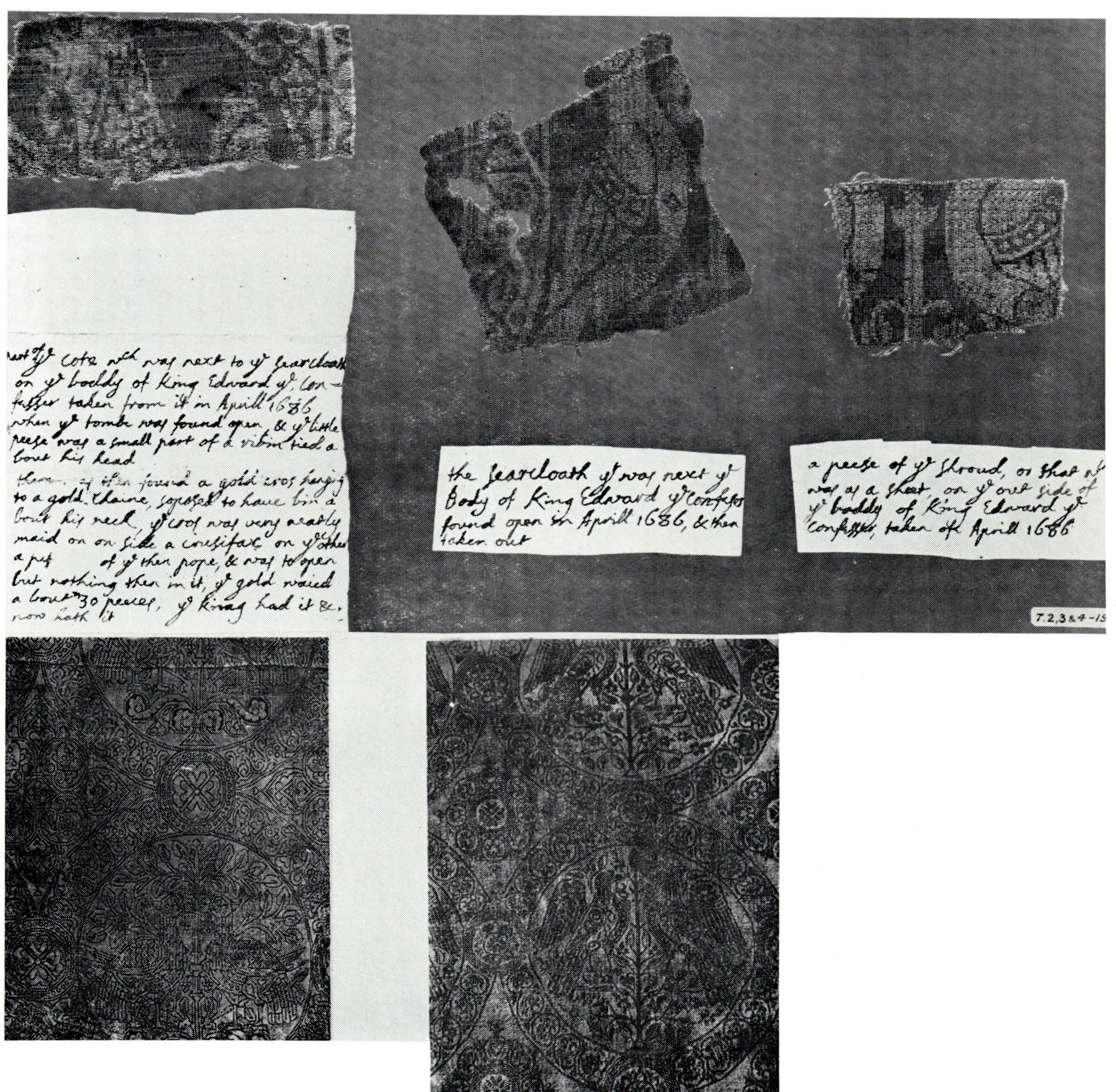

Fig. 40 (top)   FRAGMENT OF SHROUD OF EDWARD THE CONFESSOR
FROM TOMB IN WESTMINSTER ABBEY. 11TH CENTURY

Courtesy, Victoria & Albert Museum, London

Fig. 41 (bottom left)   ST. BERNARD'S CHASUBLE. 10TH–11TH CENTURY

Courtesy, Hildesheim Cathedral, Lower Saxony

Fig. 42 (bottom right)   SILK DAMASK. 12TH CENTURY

Fig. 43   ELEPHANT TISSUE IN THE RELIQUARY OF
CHARLEMAGNE IN AIX-LA-CHAPELLE
(with enlarged detail showing the woven signature)

Fig. 44   PLAIN COMPOUND TWILL. 11TH–14TH CENTURY
Courtesy, Cooper Union Museum, New York, U.S.A.

Fig. 45   FRAGMENT WITH COMPLETED PATTERN DRAWN IN. 11TH–12TH CENTURY

Courtesy, Victoria & Albert Museum, London

Fig. 46   SILK FRAGMENT. 11TH–12TH CENTURY
Courtesy, Victoria & Albert Museum, London

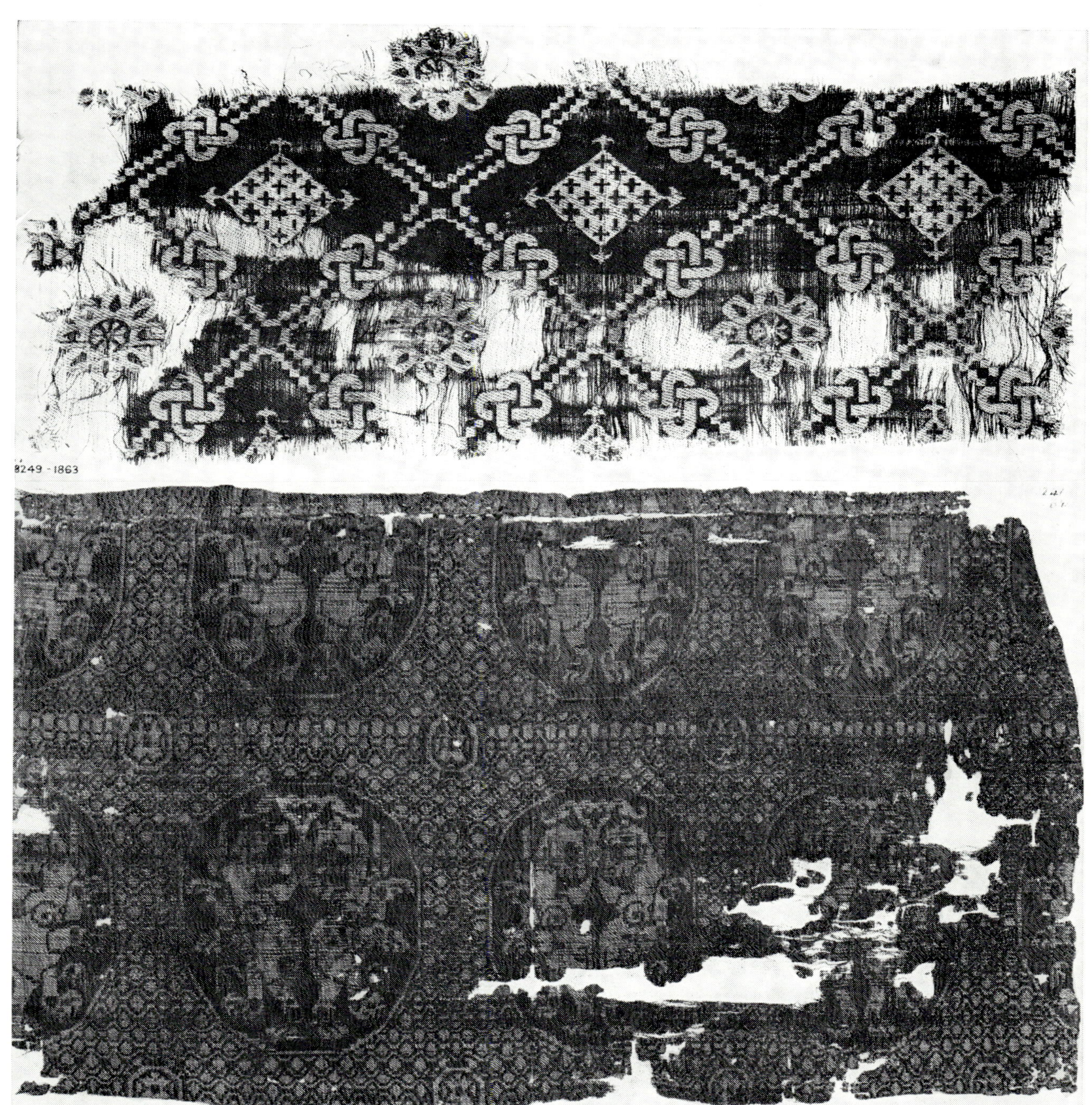

Fig. 47 (top)   SILK FRAGMENT. 11TH–12TH CENTURY
Fig. 48 (bottom)   SILK TWILL. WINGED ANIMALS WITH
CONVENTIONAL TREES. 11TH–12TH CENTURY
Courtesy of Victoria & Albert Museum, London

Fig. 49   SILK DAMASK. 11TH–12TH CENTURY
Courtesy, Victoria & Albert Museum, London

Fig. 50 SILK, WITH GRIFFINS RAMPANT & ADDORSED. 11TH–12TH CENTURY
Courtesy, Musée de Valère, Sion (Valais) Switzerland

Fig. 51   SILK FRAGMENT
Courtesy, Museo Cristiano, Vatican City, Rome

Fig. 52   SILK. FROM THE IMPERIAL WORKSHOP OF PALERMO. 12TH CENTURY
Courtesy, the Cathedral, Sens

Fig. 53　SILK DAMASK. 12TH CENTURY
Courtesy, Benedictine Monastery, Siegburg

Fig. 54, 55, 56   GRYPHON PATTERNS. 12TH CENTURY
Courtesy, Kunstgewerbe Museum, Berlin

Fig. 57   FRAGMENT OF SILK. EARLY 12TH CENTURY